The Love of a Dog

By Lindsay Thorén

Illustrated by Lisa Thorén

For Julius
and Bee

"I love the way
you are," said the boy.

"Everyone can learn
from the love of a dog."

"You show your love

every chance you get."

"You are the best
secret keeper."

"And rain or shine

you stand by my side."

"You
never get
upset

when
I make
a mess."

"You love me
no matter what."

"You always share
my excitement."

"And when you can sense
something is wrong, you
comfort me."

"Your light shines so bright,
it helps me to see my way
out of the dark."

"You make me feel safe."

"You remind
me to play,

to stay curious,

to stretch,

to go outside for fresh air,

to feel the sun on my face,

and that sometimes it's
ok to just eat and sleep."

"Your world is filled

with simple joys and wonder."

"You give me your all."

"You are the most loyal friend."

"And it seems that
no matter how much
I love you,

you love me more."

"You've taught me more than I could ever teach you," said the boy.

"Thank you for showing me what matters most."

Printed in the USA
CPSIA information can be obtained
at www.ICGtesting.com
LVHW070328231124
797044LV00023BA/30

* 9 7 9 8 8 6 9 1 1 3 6 6 5 *